OCEANS ALIVE!

Along The Shore

W
FRANKLIN WATTS
LONDON•SYDNEY

This edition first published in 2009
by Franklin Watts
Franklin Watts
338 Euston Road
London NW1 3BH

Franklin Watts Australia
Level 17/207 Kent Street
Sydney, NSW 2000

A CIP catalogue record for this book is available
from the British Library.

ISBN: 978 0 7496 9267 4

Dewey no: 577.6'99

Printed in the United States of America

Franklin Watts is a division of
Hachette Children's Books,
an Hachette UK company.
www.hachette.co.uk

Note to parents and teachers concerning
websites:
In the book every effort has been made by the
Publishers to ensure that websites are suitable for
children, that they are of the highest educational
value, and that they contain no inappropriate or
offensive material. However, because of the
nature of the Internet, it is impossible to
guarantee that the contents of these sites will
not be altered. We advise that Internet access is
supervised by a responsible adult.

For The Brown Reference Group Ltd
Project Editor: Tom Jackson
Designer: Lynne Lennon
Picture Researcher: Sean Hannaway
Indexer: Tom Jackson
Design Manager: David Poole
Managing Editor: Tim Harris
Production Director: Alastair Gourlay
Children's Publisher: Anne O'Daly
Editorial Director: Lindsey Lowe

Picture Credits
Front Cover: Shutterstock: Chad McDermott t,
Javarman c, Irabel8 b.

Alamy: Stephen Saks Photography 29; Corbis:
Theo Allofs 26-27, Sally A. Morgan 17; FLPA:
Foto Natura 19, Frans Lanting 21, Erica Olsen
16-17, Cyril Ruoso 24-25, Roger Tidman 25,
Norbert Wu 22; iStockphoto: Alexandra Draghici
11t, 11c; Natural Visions: Heather Angel 14, 14-
15; Shutterstock: Bellajay 10-11, Rich Carey 18-
19, Steve Cukrov 13, EcoPrint 23, David Hilcher
4-5, Irabel8 1b, 3b, Stephan Kerkhofs 20-21,
Chad McDermott 1t, 3t, Susan McKenzie 12,
Stephen Aaron Rees 8-9, Thomas Sztanek 6-7,
Andre van der Veen 28-29.

Artworks: The Brown Reference Group Ltd.

Contents

Introduction

Only the toughest plants and animals can survive on the shore. As you sit on a beach, watching the waves roll in, it is hard to imagine that such a peaceful place can be a tough **habitat**. You will have to watch for several hours to see why.

Rise and fall

Every day the sea level rises and falls as ocean water is pulled by the Moon's **gravity**. This up-and-down movement is called the **tides**. The tide can cover large areas of shore with water, then expose them again just a few hours later.

★ Animals and plants living in the tidal zone have to be able to live in cold, salty water – and also survive dried in the sunshine!

Highs and lows

The area affected by the tides is called the **tidal zone**. It starts at the highest point on the shore that is covered at high tide. It ends at the lowest point exposed at low tide.

Some tides are very high and then sink much lower than usual. These are **spring tides** and they affect the whole of the tidal zone. A **neap tide** is the opposite and has small rises and falls.

tidal zone

sunlit zone

★ The world's oceans can be divided into zones. Each one has a certain set of conditions.

Changing conditions

Some parts of the tidal zone are covered by water for longer than others. Other parts are mostly dry. **Organisms** along the shore have to be able to cope with the constantly changing conditions.

deep sea zone

ocean floor

Your Mission

You are going to find out more about the tidal zone and the things that live there by taking a tour of different shorelines.

Pacific Ocean

North America

1

2

3

4

South America

5

Atlantic Ocean

6

Places you will visit
1. Bay of Fundy
2. California
3. Cape Cod
4. Caribbean island
5. Suriname
6. Valdés peninsula

Big tides

The first place you visit will be the Bay of Fundy in Canada. It has the biggest tides in the world. Then you will investigate the rocky shores and sandy beaches of California, on the west coast of North America, before heading east again to explore the **salt marshes** of Cape Cod.

Warmer waters

Then you follow the Atlantic coast to the Caribbean Sea. Here, the water is warmer, and the shore life is very different.

★ Not all shorelines are the same. Rocky shores are pounded by large waves while sandy bays are calm most of the time. As a result the wildlife living in each shoreline habitat is different.

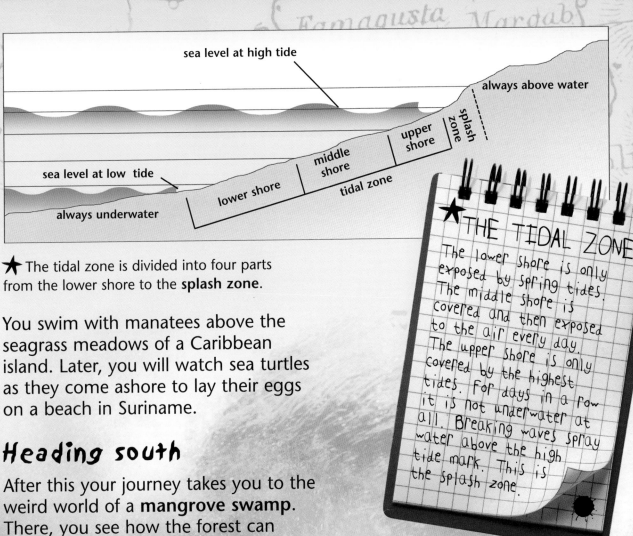

sea level at high tide

always above water

splash zone

upper shore

middle shore

sea level at low tide

lower shore

tidal zone

always underwater

⭐ The tidal zone is divided into four parts from the lower shore to the **splash zone**.

You swim with manatees above the seagrass meadows of a Caribbean island. Later, you will watch sea turtles as they come ashore to lay their eggs on a beach in Suriname.

Heading south

After this your journey takes you to the weird world of a **mangrove swamp**. There, you see how the forest can spread into the ocean and live in airless, waterlogged mud. The final stop on your mission is a very special place: the Valdés **peninsula**, in Argentina. There you will see sea lions and even giant whales living in the tidal zone.

⭐ THE TIDAL ZONE
The lower shore is only exposed by spring tides. The middle shore is covered and then exposed to the air every day. The upper shore is only covered by the highest tides. For days in a row it is not underwater at all. Breaking waves spray water above the high tide mark. This is the splash zone.

Riding the Tide

You have to travel to the Bay of Fundy in a small boat. When you arrived at the harbour several hours ago, it was low tide. Your boat was sitting on a mud bank, far below the dock wall. Now it is high tide, and the boat is floating in deep water. It is time to go.

MOON FORCE

The force that moves the tides comes from the Moon. The Moon orbits around Earth every 24 hours and its gravity pulls the ocean water into a slight bulge. One bulge faces the Moon and the other faces away. As it circles Earth, the Moon drags the bulges around with it. When a bulge moves into your part of the world, the tide rises. As it moves away, the tide falls again. The Moon causes two high tides every day, about 12 hours apart.

Going with the flow

The Bay of Fundy has the biggest **tidal range** in the world. The water level can rise by as much as 14 metres (45 feet) in six hours. That is the height of a five-storey building!

Waiting it out

As you arrive at the mouth of the bay, the tide is moving away from the shore. This is called the **ebb tide**. The Bay of Fundy's ebb tide creates a powerful stream that flows at 14 km/h (9 mph). That is too fast

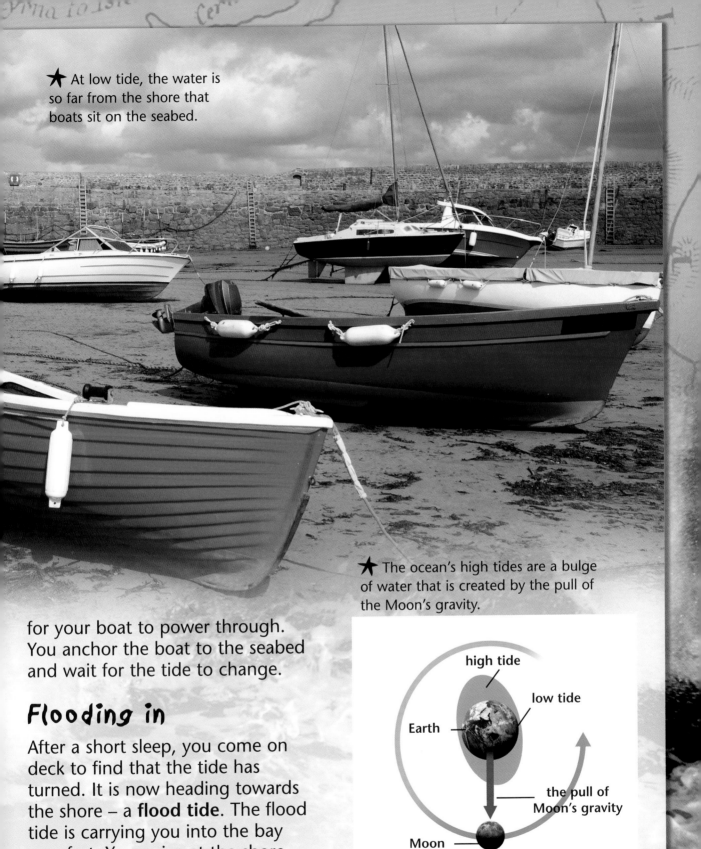

★ At low tide, the water is so far from the shore that boats sit on the seabed.

★ The ocean's high tides are a bulge of water that is created by the pull of the Moon's gravity.

high tide

low tide

Earth

the pull of Moon's gravity

Moon

for your boat to power through. You anchor the boat to the seabed and wait for the tide to change.

Flooding in

After a short sleep, you come on deck to find that the tide has turned. It is now heading towards the shore – a **flood tide**. The flood tide is carrying you into the bay very fast. You arrive at the shore just before high tide.

Pulling the Plug

Not long after you arrive, the tide starts to fall again. It is as if someone pulled the plug from a giant bath. The water drains away quickly, exposing sandy flats that gleam in the sunshine.

Warm and salty

When you reach the water you find that it is warmer than you were expecting and it is more salty, too. This is because the warm, shallow seawater is **evaporating**. When water evaporates, it leaves its salt behind. This makes the water that is left even saltier.

★ Every six hours, 115 billion tonnes (125 billion tons) of water flows in or out of the Bay of Fundy. It would take the River Thames more than a year to carry that much water!

Moving fast

As the water drains away, the sea moves back faster and faster. At times you can barely keep up. When you look back after three hours, you see that the boat you had been on at high tide is now stranded on mud, well above the level of your head. It is hard to believe that when you arrived just a few hours ago deep water covered the area. Now it is a dry beach.

Racing the tide

It takes six hours for the Bay of Fundy to drain away, and then it will refill again in another six hours. You decide to head home with plenty of time to spare. When the tide floods in, the water will rush towards the shore faster than you can run.

Hopewell Rocks

★ SHAPED ROCKS

The Hopewell Rocks have been carved into strange shapes by the Bay of Fundy's powerful tidal streams. The tops of the rocks are above the high-tide mark, and the tide has worn away below that point. Each rock is now perched on a narrower stalk of rock. One day the rocks will fall into the sea.

Rocky Pools

The weather turns bad in the Bay of Fundy, and you decide to leave. You fly to San Francisco and head for the coast. The weather is fine and it is a perfect day for exploring the rocky shore there.

Empty pools

When you get down to the bay, you find that the falling tide is slowly revealing the rocky shore. The shore is dotted with rock pools. Near the top of the shore the rock is almost bare. It is easy to walk on the shore, but there is not a lot to see in the rock pools.

Slippery shore

As you get near to the water, the rocks get slippery with green seaweed. The weed is in the pools, too. You can also see flower-like sea anemones among the plants and tiny shrimps and small crabs. Barnacles, limpets and small sea snails cling to the rocks.

★ The rocks on the lower shore are covered in more seaweed because they are exposed to the air for less time than the rocks up the shore.

Crowded together

The further down the shore you go, the more wildlife you find. The rocks near the low-tide line are covered with brown seaweed. And there are masses of mussels, sea stars and larger crabs. There are even small fish in the pools. Why do these pools have more life in them than those higher up?

Exposure time

You measure the **temperature** of the pools. The pools high on the shore are warm. They have been heated by the sunshine. Lots of the water has evaporated, too. The pool is now too warm and salty for most sea life. The lower pools are not exposed to direct sunlight for very long. They will stay cool and comfortable until the tide covers them again.

★ Starfish and sea anemones wait in a pool for the tide to come in. Anemones look like flowers but are relatives of jellyfish.

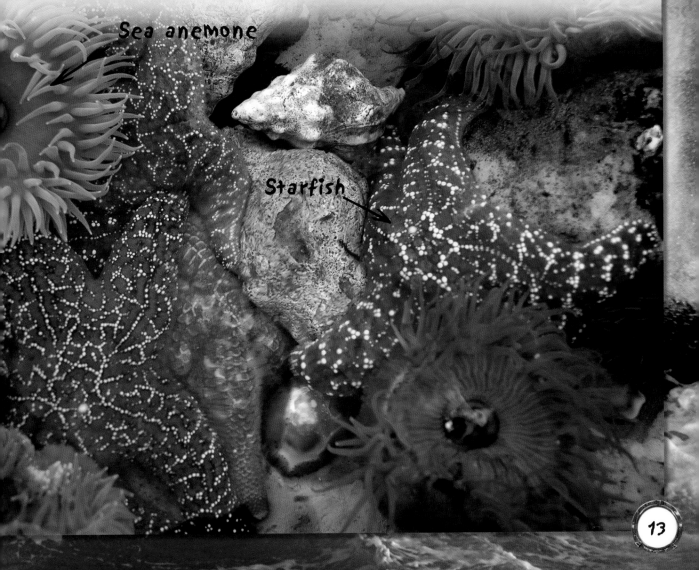

Sea anemone

Starfish

High and Dry

A lot of the animals and seaweeds on the rocky shore can live for a while out of the water completely. How do these water creatures survive exposed to the dry air?

Closing up

Most sea-shore animals get their food and **oxygen** from the water. If they are left high and dry by the falling tide, they cannot eat or even breathe properly. They survive by sealing water inside their bodies. Barnacles and mussels close up their shells. Sea anemones pull their fleshy tentacles into their soft bodies and close up like blobs of jelly. Then they wait for the tide to rise again.

★ ON THE BEACH ★
You also visit a sandy beach in California. The dunes far from the water are covered in grasses. Their roots hold the soft sand together. Further down the beach you step over the strand line, which is a heap of rubbish left by the high tide. As you near the ocean, you begin to notice small hollows that show where worms and shellfish are buried. The sand looks empty, but it is full of life.

★ A lugworm burrows into the sand. This worm eats the remains of living things mixed into the sand. It leaves pipe-shaped droppings on the surface of the sand.

Lichens

Taking places

Some animals can wait for longer than others. Mussels, for example, cannot survive out of the water for as long as barnacles. Mussels live closer to the low-tide line and are soon submerged again. Barnacles live further up the shore. Some survive in the splash zone. Up there, the animals are never under the water. They stay inside their shells until there is heavy spray from storm waves. The barnacles sift out food from these splashes.

★ Seaweeds grow in bands across the shore. Each plant is suited to surviving in a certain position in the tidal zone. **Lichens** grow in the splash zone.

Bands of life

As you look along the shore, you see that the wildlife lives in bands. Each band is home to plants and animals suited to life that distance from the low-tide mark. The further away they are, the better they are at surviving out of the water.

15

Among the Mud

The storm on the Atlantic coast is over, and you fly to Cape Cod to explore yet another type of shoreline – mud. It might not look like it but mud is full of life.

Behind the beach

At Cape Cod the sandy beaches have gaps in them. At high tide the ocean floods through these gaps into flat areas behind. The calm salty water is full of tiny mud particles, which sink to the bottom. When the tide ebbs away, it leaves behind a layer of salty mud.

★ A ringed plover probes for worms and shellfish in the mud. The bird's **prey** survive by eating the remains of dead plants and animals mixed into the mud.

★ Tough grasses and sedges grow in the mud. Their roots hold the mud together and create a salt marsh. This is a wet wilderness between the land and the sea, full of animals such as birds and crabs.

Feeding grounds

As you arrive, the mudflats are being exposed by the falling tide. Through **binoculars**, you see hundreds of shorebirds walking across the mud searching for food. What could they possibly be eating? As you squelch over the mud, the birds run away, but their food is still there. The mud is swarming with tiny snails. And when you collect a sample of mud you see it is also full of clams and worms.

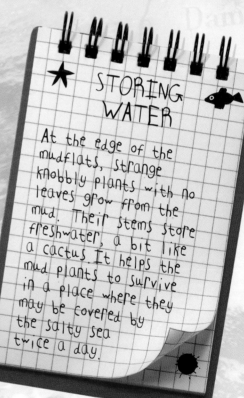

★ STORING WATER 🐟

At the edge of the mudflats, strange knobbly plants with no leaves grow from the mud. Their stems store freshwater, a bit like a cactus. It helps the mud plants to survive in a place where they may be covered by the salty sea twice a day.

Underwater Meadow

The grasses that grow on salt marshes have to survive being flooded with salt water on occasion. However, seagrasses are covered by the sea almost all the time.

Heading south

After the chilly breeze and mud of Cape Cod, you are looking forward to the next stage of your mission. The best seagrass meadows are in the warm waters of the Caribbean. The seagrass roots provide shelter for all kinds of animals, including sea urchins, lobsters and seahorses.

Octopus

★ This manatee is eating seagrass on the seafloor.

Underwater grazers

Many of the creatures living in the seagrass are hunters that prey on the fish and smaller animals. However, two of the biggest residents of the meadows – the green turtle and the manatee – feed on the seagrass itself. Manatees look like swimming pigs, but they are actually relatives of elephants. You are lucky enough to swim with some manatees as they feed in the crystal-clear water.

★ An octopus crawls through the seagrass. The meadow grows in sand made from tiny pieces of coral. The plants' roots hold the sand together and stop it getting washed away by storm waves.

Turtle Beach

During your time in the Caribbean you see lots of green sea turtles. The turtles come there to feed. Now you are going to see where they breed.

Deserted beach

After a few days at sea you are back on the beach, but this time on the wild coast of Suriname, in South America. Female turtles **mate** with the males in the ocean. Then, the females come ashore to lay their eggs in this beach's sand. Each female returns to the place where she hatched many years before. Green turtles may have used this Suriname beach for thousands of years.

★ The next part of your journey follows the sea turtles from the Caribbean Sea through the Atlantic Ocean to Suriname, on the eastern coast of South America.

★ Only female turtles travel to breeding beaches. The males stay in the seagrass.

Caribbean Sea

1

Places you will visit
1. A Caribbean island
2. Suriname

Atlantic Ocean

2

South America

★ This baby turtle is dashing for the water. Few babies make it off the beach. Crabs and birds grab them before they reach the sea.

Night visitor

You set up camp near the beach and wait for nightfall. As the sky darkens, you see a big turtle coming ashore through the surf. It takes her a long time to drag herself up the sand to the splash zone beyond the reach of the highest tides. She digs a hole in the sand with her flippers and lays about 100 eggs before covering them up and heading back to the sea.

In another nest nearby, tiny turtles are digging their way out of the sand and scuttling towards the sea. One day they will come back, too.

Mangrove Swamp

The turtle nursery lies close to a quiet shore where the sea has dumped thick layers of mud. Unlike cool Cape Cod, this mud has become more than a salt marsh. Here in the tropics the mud is home to a mangrove swamp.

★ Mangrove swamps are home to many fish, such as mudskippers. Many sea fish lay eggs among the mangrove's roots so their young have a calm and quiet place to grow.

Flooded forest

At high tide most of the mangrove is flooded. The trees seem to grow straight out of the sea. As the tide goes down, the scene becomes even stranger. The trees have roots that arch out from their trunks before disappearing into the mud. When you dig down into the salty mud itself, you find that it smells of rotten eggs. That smell tells you there is no oxygen in the mud. Mangrove roots have to take in oxygen from the air. That is why the roots arch out of ground.

★ MUDSKIPPERS

Strange little fish called mudskippers live in the mangrove swamps of the Pacific and Indian Oceans. They can breathe out of the water for a short time and use their fins to hop around on the mud. The fish can even climb trees!

Floating trees

It is impossible for seeds to grow into young mangroves in the choking mud. Instead the seeds sprout while still fixed to a branch. The **seedling** then falls off, drifts away in the water, and starts growing somewhere else.

★ The mangroves need fresh water to survive. Their roots remove the salt from the seawater. This salt forms a crust of white **crystals** on the outside of the roots.

Sea Lion Colony

It is now time to head even further south. While it was winter in Cape Cod and California, it is summer where you are heading. Sea lions and other animals will be breeding on the shore.

★ Sea lions crowd together to give birth to pups and find a mate before heading back to sea for the winter.

Breeding site

Sea lions gather on a quiet shoreline to give birth to their pups. Your destination – the Valdés peninsula in Argentina – is a good spot. You find hundreds of sea lions on the stony beach. Many of the females are feeding pups with rich milk.

Beach fight

The much bigger male sea lions do not look after pups. They are too busy fighting over mates. As you walk among the crowd of sea lions, a fight breaks out. The rivals rear up and try to bite each other. As they fight, the giant sea lions only just miss knocking you over. A pup is not so lucky – it is crushed by the fighting males.

★ A giant petrel eats a dead pup. Perhaps this one was crushed to death during a fight between males.

Whale Attack

Some of the sea lions are swimming just off the pebble beach. You are about to see one of the biggest **predators** in the world. It usually stays far out to sea. This beach is one of the few places it hunts in the tidal zone

Killer strike

Here it comes, surging through the shallows and up onto the beach. It is a killer whale, or orca. It has come to the Valdés peninsula to feast on the sea lions. It can only get close to the shore at high tide, along channels cut in the seabed by streams running down the beach.

Giant and deadly

A killer whale is as big as a van and weighs 30 times as much as the largest sea lion. Killer whales arrive at the beach in late summer. At this time, the young pups are learning to swim before heading out to sea for their first winter.

★ Killer whales normally hunt in deep water, but at this steep beach in Argentina they find meals in the shallows.

Surprise attack

The sea lions do not notice the killer approaching, but you can see its tall black fin is ploughing toward the beach. The sea lions see the whale only when it is too late. The whale powers itself onto the beach with its wide tail, snatching up a sea lion.

Smack down

The sea lion struggles to get free, but the powerful whale smacks it against the beach until it goes limp. Meanwhile, the killer has got stuck on the beach. It has to flap its great body to get back into the water. Then the whale slides away, back into the ocean to eat its meal.

Lessons We've Learned

On your mission to explore the shore line, you have found many different habitats that were home to an amazing variety of animals, but some things stayed the same.

★ Despite all the difficulties for wildlife, the tidal zone is one of richest habitats in the ocean – and anywhere on Earth.

Common factors

On every shore that you have visited, the rising and falling tides created a shifting border between the land and the ocean. This zone is very rich in food, swept in from the ocean as well as off the land.

Difficult life

Despite all the food, animals need to be specialised to survive on the shore. Life in the tidal zone is difficult, with battering waves, tumbling rocks, shifting sands and tides that leave them high and dry, hot and cold, and covered in salt twice a day.

The animals that have evolved to meet the challenge of life in the tidal zone are able to breed in huge numbers. A rocky headland may be home to millions of barnacles, and a muddy beach conceals billions of worms.

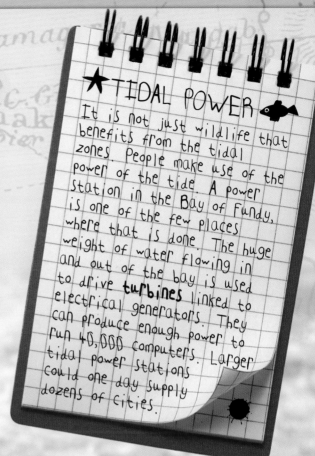

★ TIDAL POWER

It is not just wildlife that benefits from the tidal zones. People make use of the power of the tide. A power station in the Bay of Fundy, is one of the few places where that is done. The huge weight of water flowing in and out of the bay is used to drive **turbines** linked to electrical generators. They can produce enough power to run 40,000 computers. Larger tidal power stations could one day supply dozens of cities.

★ The Annapolis Basin power station harnesses the power of the huge tide in the Bay of Fundy.

Glossary

binoculars A device that lets you see things in the distance close up.

crystals Gem-like structures formed naturally by substances, such as salt.

ebb tide When the tide is flowing away from the shore.

evaporating Turning to vapour, or gas. When water turns to water vapour, it is evaporating.

flood tide When the tide is flowing towards the shore.

gravity Force of attraction that pulls things towards planets and moons.

habitat Place that provides the right food, shelter and other needs for animals.

lichen A plant-like organism that contains both fungi (related to mould) and tiny algae.

mangrove swamp A forest that grows in the tidal zone in parts of the world that are warm and wet all year around.

mate When males and females come together to make eggs or young.

neap tide A tide with a small tidal range; the opposite of a spring tide.

orbit Travel around a star, planet or moon in space.

organism Living thing. All plants and animals are organisms.

oxygen The invisible gas in the air that animals and plants must breathe in to power their bodies.

peninsula An area of land that sticks out into the sea and is surrounded by water on three sides.

predator Animal that hunts and kills another for food.

prey Animals that are killed and eaten by other animals.

salt marsh Grassy swamp that forms on a mudflat in cool salt water.

seedling A very young tree.

splash zone Part of the shore above the high tide line that is splashed by salt water.

spring tide An extreme tide that pushes the water high up the land and then pulls it far from the shore. The opposite type of tide is a neap tide.

strand line A line of debris that is left on the shore by the falling tide.

temperature A measure of how hot something is.

tidal stream Sideways flow of water created by a rising or falling tide.

tide The rise and fall in sea level. Tidal shores are those affected by tides.

tidal range Difference in height between high and low tides.

tidal zone The part of the ocean that is affected by the tides.

turbine Fan-like device that rotates when liquid or gas flows through it.

Further Information

Books

The Seashore: Usborne Spotters Guide by Su Swallow. London: Usborne Publishing, 2006.

Eyewitness: Seashore by Steve Parker. London: Dorling Kindersley, 2003.

Web sites

Games and videos from the BBC's Blue Planet site.
http://www.bbc.co.uk/nature/blueplanet/

National Oceanic and Atmospheric Administration Ocean Explorer.
http://oceanexplorer.noaa.gov/

Videos, pictures and information on the green sea turtle.
http://www.arkive.org/green-turtle/chelonia-mydas/

Watch the Bay of Fundy's tidal bore – a tidal wave that surges up the bay.
http://www.youtube.com/watch?v=7z5hxPdhtvg/

Index